T0380850

Sacred Affirmations For
Healing

STAR HALEY

To order additional copies of this book, contact:
Xlibris
1-888-795-4274
www.Xlibris.com
Orders@Xlibris.com

NOTES and INSIGHT Designed by Star Haley c1999, 2010

Thank You

William Alexander Haley
for loving me.

General Collin Powell and General Joseph Cillo
for being role models.

Colonel F. Rice and Colonel D. Gresham
for being my sister soldiers.

Department of Veterans Affairs for support.

Former Lt. Governor Michael S. Steele
for honoring my creativity.

Ambassador/Attorney/Uncle George Haley
for believing in me.

J
for reawakening my soul…

Each person who crossed my path
for the life lessons.

God…

Trust The Spirit

Dedication

To my family,
Love.

To my beloved country
Remember who we are; set the standard!

To My Fellow Veterans
Thank you for your service and for keeping America safe.

To Humanity,
Peace.

Da and Ma, thank you for life!
Wayne, Dorothy, Waco, Alma, and Andrea;
thank you for sharing the journey.
Your voices help me speak.
Rest in the arms of the Ancestors.

We will meet again…

Contents

About The Sacred Affirmations

The Sacred Affirmations are born from my struggle. Rather, my preparation to guide and support you on your journey to wellness.

While this book bears my name, the affirmations come from God. Each day, they come through me. I simply write them down as I hear them—unedited. They are more than words. The sounds caught in the rhythm of the words, are healing and the words restore divine order.

Truth is just truth, simple and pure. Be open, receive all that you need or require. In sharing the Sacred Affirmations with you, I honor God and fulfill my divine purpose.

How To Use The Sacred Affirmations

Spirit speaks, Be attentive. Listen.

Sit quietly, breathe deeply, mediate, pray, set the stage for healing your way.

Read the affirmations silently, then out loud. Live them. Give them a place in your soul. They will heal you.

Review where you are in this moment. Count your Blessings. Then, answer the questions, what do you need for balance, for peace, and for love? Why are you here? Allow the affirmations to guide you towards fulfillment — ultimate wellness.

For insight, write the thoughts that come on the journal pages that are provided. Review this information and act accordingly. When needed, repeat the process and reread your journal notes. Act!

Remember you were born in the image of God; however you define your higher power. All else is but an illusion. There is no separation or lack. We create inbalance when we submit to the way of the world.

Take a photo of yourself — your life. Look at it and assess where you are today. Six months from now, take another photo and assess where you are. Note the difference. What changed, if anything and why? What needs to change for ultimate wellness? Do the work. Celebrate the results. Give thanks.

Pay you karmic debt and move on. Don't run from life — the world. Rather require it to celebrate the gifts that you bring with an open mind and open heart. Face your fears, they are but illusions. What you tell yourself instead of listening to God.

Let go and Let God. Live! Affirm . . .

Faith

A child is born full of love and laughter.
Life happens. Innocence fades.

Trials and tribulations moves us from the inside out.
We lose our sense of self.

Blinded by the pain, we crave acceptance
and surrender our will to the will of others.
Self doubt becomes our mantra.

Ah, but God is watching.
Angels appear.
We breathe, reach towards the heavens, fold our hands in prayer.

The crooked is made straight.
Destiny unfolds.
Your greatness cannot wait.
Faith has made the whole.

For we walk by Faith, not by sight.
2 Corinthians 5:7

NOTES AND INSIGHTS

_____

_____

_____

_____

_____

_____

_____

_____

_____

_____

_____

_____

_____

_____

_____

_____

_____

_____

_____

Rejoice

Life often gives us reasons to doubt ourselves;
to question our God.
Hold fast to your faith.
Trust God.
In your darkest moment,
give thanks for all your blessings.
Count them and rejoice in them.
Then, look beyond the moment and find the blessings
disguised as a challenge or even a loss.
Take a deep breath.
Pray, ask for divine guidance. Listen!
Know with a certainty that destiny is unfolding as it should.
Know that the challenge you face is but a growth moment.
Learn the lesson. Dismiss the pain.
Remember that God is in charge.
Prepare to take the next step on your path. Move on!

Rejoice in the Lord always...
Philippians 4:4

NOTES AND INSIGHTS

_____

_____

_____

_____

_____

_____

_____

_____

_____

_____

_____

_____

_____

_____

_____

_____

_____

_____

_____

_____

_____

_____

_____

Vulnerable:
I Shake Within My Soul

I shake within my soul
as I watch the fade of all things old.
I shake within my soul
as I reach for fool's gold.
I shake within my soul
as my story goes untold.
I shake within my soul
as destiny unfolds.
I shake within my soul
as my spirit cries.
I shake within my soul
cause the eagle dies.
I shake within my soul
with the shifting of the sand.
I shake within my soul
cause I put my trust in man.
I shake within my soul
as I read the master plan.
I shake within my soul
as I heed God's command.

He set the earth on its foundations, so that it should never be moved.
Psalm 104:5

NOTES AND INSIGHTS

_____

_____

_____

_____

_____

_____

_____

_____

_____

_____

_____

_____

_____

_____

_____

_____

_____

_____

_____

Knowing

There is a certain knowing that blow breath in me.
There is a certain knowing that sets my heart at ease.
There is a certain knowing that brings the summer's breeze.
There is a certain knowing that returns the flowers and the leaves.
There is a certain knowing that brings the stars to the sky.
There is a certain knowing that connects you and I.
There is a certain knowing that breaks forth the sunrise.
There is a certain knowing that directs the moon and the tides.
There is a certain knowing that's a blessing in disguise.
There is a certain knowing that wipes the tears from my eyes.
There is a certain knowing that makes believing true.
There is a certain knowing that controls all I do.
There is a certain knowing that's called the God in you.

For I know the plans I have for you, "says the Lord…
Jeremiah 29:11

NOTES AND INSIGHTS

_____

_____

_____

_____

_____

_____

_____

_____

_____

_____

_____

_____

_____

_____

_____

_____

_____

_____

I Took A Chance On You

Even when the world frowned at you
I held your hand and smiled with you.
I took a chance on you.

Even when those who vowed to love you turned their back on you
I healed your pain and was there for you.
I took a chance on you.

Even when you fell from grace
I willingly shared my sacred space.
I took a chance on you.

Even when your funds were low
I keep the flame of hope aglow.
I took a chance on you.

Even when you were ailing
I held you tight and keep your heart from failing.
I took a chance on you.

Even though I said "I Do"
I gave my precious love to you.
I took a chance on you.

Even when you broke my heart
I stood beside you and played the part.
I took a chance on you.

Even though my star was bright
I laid beside you and shared the night.
I took a chance on you.

Even when you left me hanging
I caught the strings upon which our love was dangling.
I took a chance on you.

Even when you flaunted women in my face
I stood by you with amazing grace.
I took a chance on you.

Even when you took back the gift you gave
I gently demonstrated how a friend should behave.
I took a chance on you.

Even when you killed my trust
I stood beside you, helped clear the dust.
I took a chance on you.

Even when you got lost in the crowd
I gave more understanding than a fool's allowed.
I took a chance on you.

Even when you made me wait
when you needed me, I did not hesitate.
I took a chance on you.

Even when you _____
I won't.
Because, from now on I'm taking a chance on me.

For you do not know what tomorrow will bring...
James 4:14

NOTES AND INSIGHTS

_____

_____

_____

_____

_____

_____

_____

_____

_____

_____

_____

_____

_____

_____

_____

_____

_____

_____

_____

Drama Queens

Watch out for the drama queens and crazy makers
where there is peace
they will confuse.

Where there is pain
they exploit it.

Where there is joy
they forsake it.

Where there is love
they mistake it.

Where there is light
they remove it.

Where there is hope
they lose it.

Only let us hold true to what we have attained.
Philippians 3:16

Sacred Affirmations for Healing **Drama Queens**

NOTES AND INSIGHTS

_____

_____

_____

_____

_____

_____

_____

_____

_____

_____

_____

_____

_____

_____

_____

_____

_____

_____

_____

Is It Love?

Gaze into the eyes of those who profess to love you.
Peer into their soul.
Understand their mind.

Take time to know their rhythm.
Feel their vibrations.
Harmonize with their spirit.

Answer the questions.
Can they love you while you fulfill your destiny?
Can you love them and be all that God intended you to be?
Remember:
Love does not bargain.
Love does not compete.
Love does not retreat.

Being alone can be tough.
Saying no can be rough.
Love, but let no man mess with God's stuff.

**And now abides faith, hope, love, these three; but the greatest
of these is love.
1 Corinthians 13:13**

NOTES AND INSIGHTS

_____
_____
_____
_____
_____
_____
_____
_____
_____
_____
_____
_____
_____
_____
_____
_____
_____
_____
_____

Soul Mates

Journeys of the soul
begin in the heart.

Sealed by sacred vows
to death do us part.

Rituals honor the spirits
remember destiny.

Friends and family gather
create community.

Children born
continue humanity.

Love spoken
announce eternity…
Fulfills destiny.

Two are better than one…
Ecclesiastes 4:9-12

NOTES AND INSIGHTS

_____

_____

_____

_____

_____

_____

_____

_____

_____

_____

_____

_____

_____

_____

_____

_____

_____

_____

_____

I See Life In You

I see life in you.
Erase the pain.
Eliminate the blue.

I see life in you.
Get Up!
Keep going.
Do what you have to do.

I see life in you. I see life in you.
When faced with life's challenges
to thy own self be true.

I see life in you.
Say "I do."
Through your love – new life is born.
Go ahead, pass life on.

I see life in you.
Give what you have to give.
And, don't forget to forgive.

I see life in you.
Know that the race is already won.
For God gave his only begotten son.

I see life in you.
When faced with a fading sun.
Just let go and chant, Thy will be done.

. . . That you may have eternal life.
1 John 5:13

NOTES AND INSIGHTS

_____

_____

_____

_____

_____

_____

_____

_____

_____

_____

_____

_____

_____

_____

_____

_____

_____

_____

_____

_____

_____

Can't Go Home Anymore

Where are the landmarks that lead to the heart?
Where are the signposts that spell the words I use to boast?
Where are the friends I use to toast?
Where is the tree that use to shade me?
Where are the mom and dad who made me?
Where is the home that use to shelter me?
Where are the words that use to comfort me?
Where is grandma who use to scold me?
Where are the arms that use to hold me?
Can't go home anymore.

**...For you, O Lord have spoken, and with your blessing shall the house of
your servant be blessed forever.
Samuel 7:29**

NOTES AND INSIGHTS

_____

_____

_____

_____

_____

_____

_____

_____

_____

_____

_____

_____

_____

_____

_____

_____

_____

Touch

Be careful how you think and move.
You are programming your cells.
Thus, your reality.

Your mind, body, soul and spirit need nurturing.
Think positive thoughts.
Practice healthy nutrition.
Move skillfully – exercise.

Dance the dance of the phoenix.
Soar with the eagles.
Listen to your inner voice.

Visualize what you want.
Act like it.
Believe…pray…claim it!

Touch.
Touch only that which is pure and clean.

Touch not mine anointed. And do my prophets no harm.
Psalm 105:15

Sacred Affirmations for Healing **Touch**

NOTES AND INSIGHTS

_____

_____

_____

_____

_____

_____

_____

_____

_____

_____

_____

_____

_____

_____

_____

_____

_____

_____

_____

_____

_____

Dance

Dance.
Dance with the winds of change.
Let go and let God.

Swirl, swirl in the rhythm of balance.
Lift, lift as high as you can… then some.
Bend, bend with the curves that are thrown at you.

Catch, even catch a few.
Throw, throw some back.
Place, place the best curve on the mantle of perpetual lessons.

Recognize. Recognize. Recognize
Harmonize. Harmonize. Harmonize.
Maximize. Maximize. Maximize.
Survive… Actualize!

Let them praise his name with the dance…
Psalm 149:3

NOTES AND INSIGHTS

_____

_____

_____

_____

_____

_____

_____

_____

_____

_____

_____

_____

_____

_____

_____

_____

_____

_____

_____

Think About God

Today I will think about God instead of my problems.
Go within to your sacred place.
And, God's comforting words dry your eyes.

Listen to the sounds of joy
overshadow tormenting voices that annoy
while God's angels stand ready to deploy.

Let go of chances missed.
Release the pain and mental strain.
Remember, God's promise runs through your veins.

Taste the sweetness of holy bliss.
Seal tomorrow with a sacred kiss.
For with God, success is not a risk.

Think God.
Thank God.

The things that are impossible with men are possible with God.
Luke 18:27

NOTES AND INSIGHTS

Create

Create.
When we are happy, we create.
When we create, we are free.

Create.
When we are happy and free
we are who God meant us to be.

Create.
Fulfill your destiny.
Leave your thumb print on humanity.

Create.
When shame and pain bring you to your knees
or broken promises makes your heart freeze.

Create.
Think "at ease."
God will be pleased.

Create in me a pure heart, Oh God, and renew your spirit within me.
Psalm 51:10

NOTES AND INSIGHTS

_____

_____

_____

_____

_____

_____

_____

_____

_____

_____

_____

_____

_____

_____

_____

_____

_____

Shades Of Time

In the dust of time I search for yesterday.
In the dark of night I dream a new reality.
In the light of day I see tomorrow.
In the break of dawn I find my way.

To everything there is a season, and a time to every purpose under heaven.
Ecclesiastes 3:1

NOTES AND INSIGHTS

_____

_____

_____

_____

_____

_____

_____

_____

_____

_____

_____

_____

_____

_____

_____

_____

_____

_____

_____

Heaven Bound

When I sit beneath the mountain
and hear the howler of the wind
I am heaven bound.

When I touch the sacred
and walk in holy places
I am heaven bound.

When I feel the heartbeat
of the shadow
I am heaven bound.

When I cool from flowing water
and turn away a frown
I am heaven bound.

When I look behind the mask
and still have a second chance
I am heaven bound.

Let the Heavens rejoice...
Psalm 96: 11

NOTES AND INSIGHTS

_____

_____

_____

_____

_____

_____

_____

_____

_____

_____

_____

_____

_____

_____

_____

_____

_____

_____

_____

_____

_____

Sacred Space

Be still and know that I am God . . .
Psalm 46:10

This Sacred Space is provided for you to visit and raise your energy level—to heal. Simply open the book to this page, connect with God and focus on what you need to restore balance. Experience a Miracle!

Contact Star

Star Haley would like to hear from you and continue to support your healing. To share your thoughts, make a prayer request, ask for a personal healing session, or customized healing products, please visit www.starhaley.com

Star Haley is available for healing sessions, lectures, and workshops based on this book and other healing topics. Details will be sent upon request.

About the Author

Star Haley, a born healer, is a spiritual life coach, a licensed professional counselor, reiki master, and award-winning author. She is a former science teacher, planning commission chair and military officer who received a direct commission from the President of the United States to the rank of first lieutenant, with promotion to captain while serving at Pentagon. Star served as a protocol officer to the Secretary of Defense, with service at the U.S. Mission to the United Nations. Her numerous awards include being honored as an "Outstanding Young Woman in America."

Star is a gifted dreamer and visionary who turns dreams into reality. One of her dreams became a landark doctoral dissertation with information from NASA and other space agencies on the multicultural and interpersonal dynamics during long-duration spaceflight and interplanetary migration.

Star worked with her life partner of 36 years, W. Alex Haley, son of Alex Haley, the author of Roots, to create the Alex Haley Museum and served as its curator. She spearheaded the Sister City relationship between the Gambia West Africa and Annapolis, Maryland; Kunta Kinte's arrival point in America and supported the development of the Alex Haley memorial at the City Dock of Annapolis, Maryland. She is the founder and executive director of the Roots Institute. Also, she served as the Chair the Annapolis Maryland Planning Commission and directed the development of the city's comprehensive plan.

Her publications include numerous federal and military technical reports. Her contributions to the Official Black History Month Kit are the publications: *Alex Haley: God's Story Teller and Some Prominent Black Women in the Struggle for Education.* Also, she developed the Department of Defense publication *Women in America's Defense.* Her exhibits include the Pentagon's *Prisoners of War and Missing in Action Corridor*, the *Hispanic Medal of Honor Winners;* installed in the Hall of Heroes, and *History In The Making*, a traveling exhibit on the life of Michael S. Steele, former Chair of the Republican National Committee and Lieutenant Governor of Maryland. Her next exhibit, *Hero of Justice*, will honor the life of former Ambassador of the Gambia, West Africa, and Attorney George W. Haley.

Star brings together her spiritual anointing, training, and experiences to help humanity heal and evolve. Her *divine purpose is to help humanity heal and transition to living in outer space.*